I Only Have Eyes For You...

PUBLISHED BY MQ PUBLICATIONS LIMITED
12 THE IVORIES, 6–8 NORTHAMPTON STREET
LONDON N1 2HY
TEL: +44 (0) 20 7359 2244
FAX: +44 (0) 20 7359 1616

EMAIL: MAIL@MQPUBLICATIONS.COM
WEBSITE: WWW.MQPUBLICATIONS.COM

DESIGN: PHILIPPA JARVIS
EDITOR: LEANNE BRYAN

ISBN: 1-84072-601-6

10 9 8 7 6 5 4 3 2 1

PRINTED AND BOUND IN CHINA

I Only Have Eyes For You...

David Baird

MQP

Are the stars out tonight?
I don't know if it's cloudy or bright,
'Cause I only have eyes for you, dear.

Al Dubin

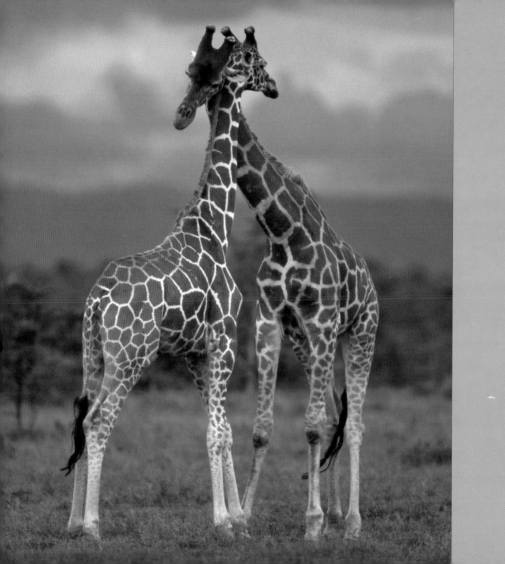

Twined together and, as is
   customary,
For words of rapture groping, they
"Never such love," swore, "ever
   before was!"
Contrast with all loves that
   had failed or staled
Registered their own as
   love indeed.
Robert Graves

7

I dare not ask a kiss,
I dare not beg a smile,
Lest having that, or this,
I might grow proud the while.

No, no, the utmost share
Of my desire shall be
Only to kiss that air
That lately kissèd thee.

Robert Herrick

Drink to me only with thine eyes,
And I will pledge with mine;
Or leave a kiss but in the cup
And I'll not look for wine.

Ben Jonson

Put tacks in my shoes,
Feed me vinegar juice,
And do other mean, bad,
  awful stuffsky.
But promise me this:
I won't die without
Kissing my glorious
  Lizzie Pitofsky.

Judith Viorst

In the sweetness of friendship let there be laughter, and sharing of pleasures.

Kahlil Gibran

Love shall be our token; love be yours and love be mine.

Christina Rossetti

It is the passion that is in a kiss that gives to it its sweetness; it is the affection in a kiss that sanctifies it.

Christian Nevell Bovee

I dream of you to wake;
would that I might
Dream of you and not
wake but slumber on.

Christina Rossetti

Oh, beautiful are the flowers
   of your garden,
The flowers of your garden are fair:
Blue flowers of your eyes
And dusk flower of your hair;
Dew flower of your mouth
And peony-budded breasts,
And the flower of the curve of
   your hand
Where my hand rests.

Helen Hoyt

No man sees far, most see no farther than their noses.

Thomas Carlyle

He took the bride
about the neck
And kissed her lips
with such a
clamorous smack
That at the parting
all the church
did echo.

William Shakespeare

Love means the body,
the soul, the life, the
entire being. We feel
love as we feel the
warmth of our blood,
we breathe love as we
breathe air, we hold it
in ourselves as we hold
our thoughts. Nothing
exists for us.

Guy de Maupassant

I have great hopes that we shall love each other all our lives as much as if we had never married at all.

Lord Byron

—All my life I've been waiting for someone, and when I find her, she's a fish.
—Nobody said love is perfect.

Tom Hanks and John Candy,
from "Splash"

I would love to spend all my time writing to you; I'd love to share with you all that goes through my mind, all that weighs on my heart, all that gives air to my soul; phantoms of art, dreams that would be so beautiful if they could come true.

Luigi Pirandello

The eyes are not responsible when the mind does the seeing.

Publilius Syrus

How do I love thee?
Let me count the ways.
I love thee to the depth
and breadth and height
My soul can reach…

Elizabeth Barrett Browning

A kiss is a lovely trick designed by nature to stop speech when words become superfluous.

Ingrid Bergman

Oh! Death will find me, long before I tire Of watching you…

Rupert Brooke

False friendship, like the ivy, decays and ruins the walls it embraces; but true friendship gives new life and animation to the object it supports.

Sir Richard Burton

Was this
the face that
launched
a thousand
ships, and
burnt the
topless towers
of Ilium?

Christopher Marlowe

If I could write words
Like leaves on an
      autumn forest floor
What a bonfire my
      letters would make.
If I could speak words
      of water
You would drown
      when I said
"I love you".

Spike Milligan

49

When, full of warm and eager love,
I clasp you in my fond embrace,
You gently push me back and say,
"Take care, my dear,
   you'll spoil my lace."

William Wetmore Story

Love does not consist in gazing at each other, but in looking outward together in the same direction.

Antoine de Saint-Exupéry

The eyes those silent tongues of love.

Miguel de Cervantes

A kiss, when all is said, what is it?
A rosy dot placed on the "i" in loving;
'Tis a secret
Told to the mouth instead of to the ear.

Edmond Rostand

Oh how sweet it is to hear one's own convictions from another's lips.

Johann Wolfgang von Goethe

And they called it puppy love
Oh, I guess they'll never know
How a young heart really feels
And why I love her so.

Paul Anka

I wonder what fool it was that first invented kissing.

Jonathan Swift

Why does a man take it for granted that a girl who flirts with him wants him to kiss her—when, nine times out of ten, she only wants him to want to kiss her?

Helen Rowland

Reproof on her lips, but a smile in her eyes.

Samuel Lover

In love, there is always one who kisses and one who offers the cheek.

French proverb

Come live with
me, and be
my Love,
And we will all
the pleasures
prove.

Christopher Marlowe

Camerado, I give you
my hand!
I give you my love more
precious than money,
I give you myself before
preaching or law;
Will you give me yourself?

Walt Whitman

I love him, I love him, ran the patter of her lips And she formed his name on her tongue and sang.

Carl Sandburg

When love and skill work together, expect a masterpiece.

John Ruskin

...then I did the simplest thing in the world. I leaned down... and kissed him. And the world cracked open.

Agnes de Mille

Those whom true love has held, it will go on holding.

Lucius Annaeus Seneca

Come, cuddle your head on my
   shoulder, dear,
Your head like the golden-rod,
And we will go sailing away
   from here
To the beautiful land of Nod.

Ella Wheeler Wilcox

And still they gazed, and still the wonder grew, That one small head could carry all he knew.

Oliver Goldsmith

My heart is a bargain today. Will you take it?

W. C. Fields

If passion drives you, let reason hold the reins.

Benjamin Franklin

'Tis said of love that it sometimes goes, sometimes flies; runs with one, walks gravely with another; turns a third into ice, and sets a fourth in a flame: it wounds one, another it kills: like lightning it begins and ends in the same moment: it makes that fort yield at night which it besieged but in the morning; for there is no force able to resist it.

Miguel de Cervantes

A thing of beauty is a
　　joy for ever:
Its loveliness increases;
　　it will never
Pass into nothingness;
　　but still will keep
A bower quiet for us,
　　and a sleep
Full of sweet dreams...

John Keats

Many waters cannot quench love, neither can the floods drown it.

Song of Solomon